Practic

PATIO GARDENING

Yvonne Rees

The Crowood Press

First published in 1993 by
The Crowood Press Ltd
Ramsbury, Marlborough
Wiltshire SN8 2HR

British Library Cataloguing in Publication Data

A catalogue record for this book is available from the British
Library

ISBN 1 85223 735 X

Picture Credits

Line-drawings by Claire Upsdale-Jones

For the use of photographs, thanks are due to the following:
Briastone/R.S. Trippier, pages 36 and 45 (top right); Britannic,
pages 39 and 40; Brynphotos, opposite and pages 1, 12, 17
and 43; Chilstone Garden Ornaments, pages 42 and 51; Dave
Pike, pages 31, 47, 57 and 61; Sheila Fitzjones, page 10 (top
left); Froyle Pottery, page 33 (top); J P Communications Ltd,
page 7; Larchlap, page 33 (bottom); Pelicans P.R., page 10
(bottom right); Yvonne Rees, pages 13 (bottom left), 15,
18–19, 23, 25, 27 (top), 29 and 49; Yvonne Rees/Chelsea
Flower Show, page 13 (bottom right); Unwins Seeds Ltd, pages
21, 24, 27 (bottom), 37, 44, 45 (bottom left) and 60; and
Michael and Lois Warren, page 32.

Typeset in Optima by Chippendale Type Ltd,
Otley, West Yorkshire
Printed and bound in Great Britain by
BPCC Hazell Books, Aylesbury

CONTENTS

INTRODUCTION

Patio, courtyard, back yard — whatever name we choose to call it, that sun-blessed paved area, however small, can be our own little slice of paradise. With its sheltered, usually sunny aspect and hard surface that ensures the area remains relatively clean and dry, here is a pleasant place to sit out at virtually any time of the year. Even planning and equipping the patio can be a pleasure, with its decorative paving, protective screens, furniture, features and accessories. It is quite as much fun as interior decorating, but with the bonus of plants in all their wide variety of shape, form and colour, to mix and match into an ever-changing display through the seasons.

We all love the idea of this 'outdoor living area', which is sheltered and stylish for lazy summer afternoons or fun evening barbecues. However, some may find the prospect of hard landscaping — that is, the actual building work involved — a bit daunting. Yet if a little care is taken planning and a methodical approach used in construction, this side of th need not be a problem — indeed, with design possibilities these days it might be an exciting and enjoyable challenge.

You could create a kind of instant with loose-laid timber decking instea cemented slabs, and free-standing sect of trellis or screening. By adding a care chosen selection of dramatic plant attractive containers, your patio coul completed in an afternoon. This migh an excellent way to breathe new life int existing but rather drab patio, or coul used to transform somewhere you do intend to stay long as the whole pac can be packed away and taken with when you move. Perhaps you are afra the cost — the finished effect can cert look expensive and is somehow redole a leisurely and sophisticated lifestyle —

Even a small balcony can be transformed into a patio — the perfect place to sit and enjoy the sunshine and to grow a few plants in pots.

:e the most of limited space in towns and cities by converting a flat roof into a delightfully
uded patio.

do all or some of the work yourself and recycled or inexpensive materials in a ative way, costs can be kept right down the finished effect will be all the more vidual for the little extra effort involved.

ecause a patio is semi-enclosed or, at t, clearly defined from the rest of the Jen and moderate to minute in size, it be planned on a manageable scale, er for your imagination or your pocket. e dreams can come true: if the site is a draughty, it can be protected by ens, fencing or hedging; if it is too large encourage that necessary sense of pri-y and intimacy, divide it up with parti-s or screens of climbing plants. Is the too small? A clever use of mirrors, npe-l'oeil and colour co-ordinated ting schemes can work magic in mak-a small patio look larger. Because a o is private and secluded, you can

choose virtually any style and atmosphere without it looking incongruous. It may be that your fantasy is a country cottage garden: re-create that feeling on your patio with herring-bone brick, tubs of old-fashioned plants and a traditional bench. Alternatively go for a Mediterranean atmosphere with lots of terracotta, dramatic aromatic plants and a large umbrella over the picnic table. Others might yearn for the understated simplicity of an oriental garden, and will use raked sand, a few strategically placed boulders and an exquisite arrangement of evergreens.

A patio will increase your use of your garden on cooler, damper days; with lighting you will be able to enjoy it at night too. Perhaps we should therefore view it not as losing a part of the garden to paving, but instead as gaining a wonderful extension to our living space.

1 • PLANNING AND SITING

The patio serves many purposes: it acts as a visual and physical link between the house and garden; it is a private place for enjoying a little sunny solitude; and it is a paved area that is practical enough for dining and lounging furniture. It also offers the gardener his or her main opportunity to devise some creative planting plans in pots, tubs and other containers. Naturally, you will want the feature to be a success on all these counts, and this is where a little pre-planning can make all the difference between a rather glum and draughty patch of paving, and a true outdoor living area that is a pleasure to use all the year round.

A little forethought and careful planning will also help with the choice and ordering of the necessary materials. For example, you are less likely to purchase far more slabs or bricks than you need if you have worked the design out in advance to scale on graph paper. Or should your budget not run to meet your patio dreams, plans are more easily amended – often for the better – before the project is tackled, than if you change horses in mid-project. Size, style, practicalities and even position must be well thought out before a spade is lifted or a slab laid.

Practical Pointers

It really does help if you draw your plans to scale on graph paper as this will give you some idea of the scale and cost of the project. Try to consider all the practical implications too – for example, if access to the rear of the property is limited, delivery of bulky or messy materials may be a problem. Where a mature garden is already established, you will want any damage or upheaval kept to a minimum. Are there existing drains, inspection covers or a damp-proof course in an adjoining building to consider?

The proposed area may include a slope

or uneven ground which will have to [be] terraced or levelled. Levelling and backf[ill]ing will add considerably to your over[all] budget unless you choose to use timb[er] decking rather than pave your patio are[a.]

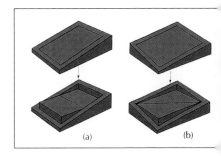

Cutting and filling to level: (a) a sloping site; (b) a tilting site.

Timber decking is flexible enough to co[pe] with changes of level without being trem[en]dously expensive, and it is easily remov[ed] should you decide to change the style [or] purpose of the area. Remember that w[hile] patios should be warm and sheltered, t[hey] should also be private – will this involve [the] erection of screens, fences or trellis-wo[rk] or could an existing wall or similar struct[ure] be used?

Making a Start

Books, magazines and gardens you h[ave] visited will have influenced your idea[s to] some extent on the type of patio you h[ope] to create. Items at your local garden ce[ntre] may also be the starting point of your pl[an.] Make a note of not just how you want [the] patio to look, but how you hope to us[e it] too. Will it be a kind of outdoor living-ro[om] with comfortable furniture, and the pl[ants] taking on the role of soft furnishings [and] accessories? Perhaps you have alw[ays] dreamed of having a permanent barbe[cue]

a with outdoor dining facilities and a
per system of garden lighting for evening
ties. Or maybe the plants will take prior-
each one to be specially chosen for its
age, flowers or scent, and with seating
uded not so much for comfort or for
esco meals as to rest and appreciate the
its better.

or some, a patio is an excuse to design
elaborate formal water garden, the
ed or sunken features linked by falls or
ercourses, and incorporating fountains
other moving water features. To look
ly attractive such features can be built to
ch the main paving material, whether
be brick, stone or timber. This idea can
extended to other hard landscaping fea-
s too, such as raised beds, built-in
ing, and patio walls and steps.

When you have a rough idea in mind of
r ideal patio, find out how it might fit
your garden. The following sections on
tion, shape and size will point you in
right direction. If you find it hard to
alize the patio on paper alone, it may
to map out the proposed features on
using pegs and string, or an old hose-
for more curvaceous outlines. Shapes
out of cardboard boxes help define the
tion of plant containers, while a few
is from the house – such as chairs and
es – may help the illusion. Walk
ngst it, to see how it works on a
tical level. Viewing the whole thing
above – say from an upper storey
low – is useful to get some perspective
e overall plan, but also consider the
ned patio from various vantage points
nd the garden to decide how well it fits
om all angles. Plans are easily altered
improved at this stage.

itioning the Patio

ctly beyond the back door is not auto-
cally the best place to site a patio,

*The patio – a dry paved area for plants and
furniture – makes the perfect link between
home and garden.*

although obviously it is the most convenient
as it offers easy access, good views from
indoors on poor weather and is an excellent
way to make the transition from home to
garden. However, if that spot is naturally
damp, dank and chilly, north-facing or
simply not very practical due to the style of
house or layout of the grounds, then do
consider siting the patio elsewhere. After
all, there is no point in taking the trouble to
design and install the feature if you are not
going to be keen to use it at every possible
opportunity.

The ideal spot should be warm and
sunny, and that may be at the far end of the
garden or even in the centre – such a patio
can make an attractive and unusual focal
point if it is thoughtfully integrated with the
rest of the garden. However, it may also be
the case that you have no choice and the
only site is less than perfect: here you must

Position your patio where it will receive maximum sunshine. Sometimes this will not be close to the house but in another part of the garden where clever planting and boundary walls may be necessary to provide the feeling of privacy.

compensate by providing good shelter and by using warm colours, perhaps developing a Mediterranean theme. If you are really up against a bleak and windy site, perhaps the area could be partially enclosed like a traditional terrace, with low brick or stone walls and a roof overhead which still allows views of the garden beyond.

Sometimes an area suggests itself for a patio – in front of a south-facing summerhouse or chalet perhaps, around a swimming pool or crowning a natural rise in the landscape. A large garden may well support several paved areas, each with its own individual character to suit its purpose. Thus there may be the perfect sun-trap for sunbathing, an eating and barbecue area, and perhaps an enclosed 'winter garden' which is at its best when the rest of the garden is dormant. A whole complex of

patios might be planned and linked, ma the garden as interesting as a serie

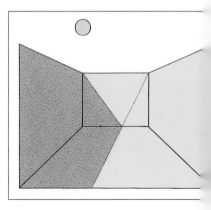

Work out the sunniest spot in the garden for positioning your patio.

Where the garden provides a natural hollow or depression, why not expand this into a sunken patio area? It may be cheaper and easier than landfilling and levelling, and it offers instant shelter and seclusion.

inating rooms, one opening on to
ther to create a wonderful and easily
ntained total scheme. Note here,
ever, that it is important that any patio
sited away from the house must be
essible by means of paths or stepping-
es in wet weather.

lternatively, if your garden is small you
not have a lot of choice where to
tion the patio, but would perhaps con-
r turning over the whole site to a sophis-
ed patio complex. This saves cutting up
area visually (which would only make it
even smaller), is easier to maintain
, with various features incorporated
in the patio format, can provide plenty
terest.

u may not have any garden to the rear
l, but a yearning for a little patch of
dise where you can sit and soak up the

sunshine may lead you to consider creating
such a theme at the front of the house (a
possibility if some privacy can be relied on),
on a balcony, or even on a roof. With high-
rise patios, however, you need to bear in
mind the problems of weight – paving,
furniture and tubs of damp soil can really
load on the kilograms even before the
weight of any occupants is taken into consideration. Timber decking may be a lighter
and, in many ways smarter, option. You
should also consider fibreglass plant containers, lighter weight composts and plastic
or aluminium furniture. There will also be
other additional problems to tackle on a
roof-top patio, such as limited access both
for the initial building materials and additional soil and water, and the extreme expo-
sure to sun and wind such sites are usually
prone to.

The well-planned patio might incorporate steps leading to the rest of the garden, built-in planting beds and attractive dining furniture as an extension of your indoor living space.

Shape and Size

The shape and size of your patio will largely be dictated by the space available, but will also depend on cost. Paving materials can be expensive over large areas, although these costs can be reduced by combining such materials with cheaper ideas and surfaces – for example, pebbles or gravél, and water or planting spaces. With larger areas, this mix of materials can be a good idea from an aesthetic angle too, as a large expanse of one type of paving can look monotonous. Alternatively, you can create patterns and designs such as borders, blocks and strips, and elaborate patterns like herring-bone and basket weave by using different colours and configurations of paving, brick and timber. Some ranges include different shapes, and shapes that

are perfect for devising intricate patte
and designs.

Avoid a straight square or rectangle sha
for your patio – although this does m.
calculating materials easier – and incorp
ate other features, curved planting beds o
change of level. The latter might take
form of raised beds, a pool edged in
matching or complementary material, st
or terracing.

Consider built-in seating, sunbath
platforms, a hot tub or spa bath, o
children's sand-pit to add variety. The l
way to break up and add interest to a
large patio – and paradoxically this m
be one in a small garden where you h
decided to take over the complete site
to divide the area into different 'roo
using screens or plantings. Thus you m
have a separate seating area, barbecue o
ner, pool complex and so on.

In a small space, your ideas are lim
only by the number of features you
include. Do not let a lack of space cra
your style, however, and take the oppor
ity of reduced material costs to really m

The gazebo is highly decorative but a useful feature for providing shade and shelter, especially on a patio in another part of the garden.

ething special of the area you have.
ate a cosy, private atmosphere, or work
tle illusory magic by including mirrors
ake effects such as doorways in your
me. Often a tiny back yard is intimi-
d by high walls – paint these white and
climbers or hanging plants, or enlist the
ices of a *trompe-l'oeil* artist to minimize
dominating effect.

de and Shelter

os are ideally draught-free, so some
of shelter will probably be necessary –
er a wall, fencing, trellis-work or
ens in a style to suit other features, or
h can quickly be clothed in climbing
ts to create a wonderful living curtain of
e, colour and possibly scent too (*see
26*). Prevailing weather conditions
determine their precise position, but
cy must be a consideration too.

Screens and trellis-work can be the most
ornamental options, and have the big
advantage of being only semi-permanent
should you be planning to move in the near
future. These come in bamboo, reeds, gras-
ses or willow hurdles for a very natural
look. Garden trellis-work can be in a simple, rustic style comprising chestnut poles
nailed together in a square or diagonal
framework; it can also be highly decorative
in stained or painted timber, incorporating
Gothic and medieval designs. Some trellises are so striking that it is almost a pity to
cover them in plants. Fencing is not generally as ornamental as trellis-work, but it is
easily and quickly erected and forms a solid
screen immediately. Lapped timber panels
afford the most privacy, but they do need a
little dressing up with plants or distracting
features to make them pleasing to the eye.

Often a wall is already in existence, and
if this is not as attractive as you might have

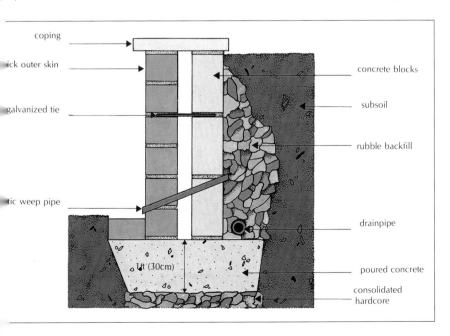

etaining walls must be built strongly and incorporate good drainage.

liked – you cannot beat the mellow effect of old, weathered brick – you can dress it up a little with climbing plants trained across trellis-work or across wires fixed directly to the wall. If you are considering a new wall, it can be highly ornamental. A low wall is often used as a divider to separate one part of the patio from another, or to create a boundary between the patio and the rest of the garden. Various block designs are available which have been designed specially for use on patios. They do create a very modern look, however, and if you prefer something a little more traditional then use bricks (which come in a variety of colours from buffs and russets to greys and blues) or build in a patterned design. For a more informal look, a drystone-wall can be planted directly with rock plants and trailing plants.

Overhead shelter can be equally important, shading plants and people not just from the occasional shower but also from the damaging effects of strong sunshine. The prettiest way to shade a patio is with a pergola – a decorative framework of brick, metal or timber, usually draped with climbing plants to produce an attractive, dappled

Honeysuckle (*Lonicera*) Probably one of best known climbing plants and, thanks to heavily scented flowers, remains a firm pat favourite. There are actually a great many different forms to suit virtually every situatic – deciduous and evergreen honeysuckles, fully hardy and frost-tender types, and flow that bloom at nearly all times of the year. Many have attractive foliage and berries as well as flowers. *L. fragrantissima*, for example, is fully hardy with narrow dark green leaves and delightfully scented crean white flowers in winter to early spring. *L. japonica* 'Aureo-reticulata' is a frost-harc evergreen which produces fragrant flowers late autumn and produces bright green lea with striking bright yellow veins.

Pergolas can be constructed in whatever materials suit the style and scale of your patio; this simple arrangement of larch poles creates an unmistakably rustic appearance.

shade. Pergola styles vary and, if prefer, can be shaded with movable ca screens. Traditionally, a large, brightly oured umbrella provides adequate sh above a table and chairs, but increas popular are Continental awnings w affix to the side of the building, and v can be electrically retracted as and v required. These come in a wide ran styles and sun-proof colours.

Putting on the Style

Getting the shape and size right will you the perfect patio framework, bu attention to style that will make a succ

...untry cobbles and the right containers ...create a cottage atmosphere.

An ornamental stone balustrade makes a fine feature between a classical patio or terrace and the rest of the garden.

...feature. Choosing to create a certain ...osphere will make it easier to select ...nts, features and accessories to suit, as ...l as pull the whole scheme together in a ...st satisfactory and professional looking ...nner.

...he style might be matched to that of an ...oining interior – a simplistic, oriental ...k for example. Or, where the patio is ...te secluded, the style might be a com-...e and surprising contrast – you may ...ire the flavour of the countryside in the ...dle of a town, for example. An old-...ioned country cottage look is easily ...tured with rustic-style paving and fea-...s, old-fashioned plant containers and ...itional cottage plants. A much more ...nal look can be created with mostly ...grated features and a limited colour

scheme – perhaps a very restful green and white, or soft pastel shades.

The sheltered environment of the patio is often perfect for growing more tender plants, and a Mediterranean-style scheme can be an exciting reminder of enjoyable holidays abroad. Terracotta pots containing exotic-looking plants such as the spiky yucca, brightly coloured geraniums and other summer blooms look stunning against a bright, white-painted wall to create a real sun-trap – finish the scene off with a table, chairs and a giant umbrella.

...ries of small troughs make a feature of ...e outside stairs.

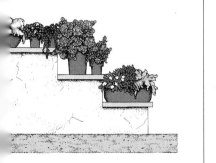

Clever use of trellis and climbing plants can create a wholly private and magically enclosed environment.

2 • BUILDING THE PATIO

By definition, your patio will comprise a firm, level surface suitable for both dry days and wet, and which is ideal for standing pots, tubs, patio furniture and accessories. There may be low walls, pools and sunken or raised beds built into the scheme too. Of all garden features, the patio requires some level of building skill – or at least an enthusiasm to try your hand at concreting, bricklaying, timber erecting or stonework. The alternative is to budget for a builder to do the job for you.

Various factors will influence your choice of style and material – how much it costs, how easy it is to lay and, of course, how it will look. The options are wide, being limited only by your imagination, and if you want to be really original you could mix and match different materials to create different patterns and designs. Do not forget, however, that other features look best if constructed, or at least faced, in a matching material. It is therefore important to have worked out the whole scheme to scale beforehand so that you know the quantities of materials to buy.

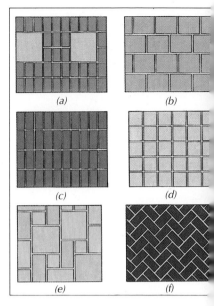

Paving slabs, stones and bricks can be laid in an infinite number of patterns to maintain interest and originality: (a) mixing concrete slabs with bricks: (b) staggering the joints when laying plain paving slabs to make them more interesting; (c) Mediterranean terracotta tiles: (d) square concrete pavers; (e) different sizes, shapes and colours produce a crazy paving effect; (f) bricks or blocks laid in a herringbone pattern.

Paving Options

Concrete

Well-laid concrete can be an inexpensive yet attractive option. It might look a bit plain over large areas, but it is easily made more decorative by adding colouring powders, or sprinkling with shingle or chippings to add extra texture and interest. Such additions are a good idea where the patio is a sun-trap as they cut down on glare. You can also vary the appearance by lightly brushing the surface with a broom while it is still wet, or leaving it to 'go off' for about eight hours before brushing it and hosing it down. You can buy special patterns which are simply stamped on to the wet concrete to produce the effect of paving slabs, or bricks, stones or pebbles can be pres[sed] into the concrete to make lines and patt[erns] and add texture too.

Paving Slabs

Preformed slabs probably form the m[ost] popular option for patio paving. They [are] available in a great many shapes and st[yles] including mock stone and brick, and [the] more expensive types are convinci[ngly] realistic yet still far cheaper than the [real] thing. Different colours, textures and i[nter]locking shapes mean that an infinite n[um]ber of patterns are possible.

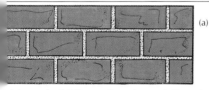

...s can be laid in a circular design to ...e a semi-formal patio, perfect for an ...of-garden site. An antique metal seat ...tly suggests an old-fashioned ...sphere.

Bricks and Tiles

Bricks can be used to create a mellow, rustic look, but also can be lined up smartly in geometric patterns to suit a slick, city back yard. They must be recommended for paving use, especially as there is a wide range of colours available from yellows and reds through to black. Quarry tiles also come in a similar colour range and are useful for creating a Mediterranean look if the patio is frost free. You might even use ceramic floor tiles if the climate permits, and here the possibilities are endless with many fantastic colours and patterns to choose from.

Stone

Natural stone – usually sandstone or lime-stone – is available in regular paving slabs or as random pieces for 'crazy paving' effects. Stone or granite sets, measuring about

...icks can be laid in a variety of ways, influencing ...oth strength and appearance: (a) stretcher ...ond – bricks laid lengthways, good for single ...af walls; (b) English bond – alternate courses of ...retchers and headers; (c) English garden wall ...ond – two or more courses of stretchers to one ...headers; (d) Flemish wall bond – one header ...d three stretchers on each course; (e) Flemish ...ond – alternate stretchers and headers on each ...urse.

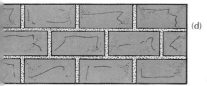

5–10 sq in (13–25 sq cm) and more usually employed in building pavements, can also be used creatively.

Cobbles

Round cobbles packed close together make an interesting change of texture on the patio, although they do create too uneven a surface for furniture. They can also be bought in square sets which make them as quick and easy to lay as paving slabs.

Gravel, Shingle and Sand

Areas of gravel, shingle or pebbles make an interesting change of texture if areas are interspersed with another more stable material. They are often seen in orie schemes where, along with raked sa they might represent a beach or desert p designed in miniature.

Timber Decking

Timber decking has become increasi popular as a surfacing material for the den. Planks are arranged in pattern create a continuous surface, and th raised several inches or sometimes sev feet above ground level by means wooden posts and joists. Where decking adjoins a house or similar build it is fastened to the wall with coach b The beauty of decking is that it can adjusted to any height or shape of area,

Using timber as a paving material offers the chance to extend your design into other features, such as built-in plant containers, changes of level and a pergola for overhead interest.

cope with any changes of level easily
inexpensively without the need for
elling or backfilling.

xtra features such as fitted furniture or
nting boxes are easily integrated, and a
e range of designs and finishes are
sible – from herring-bone and basket-
ve patterns to coloured stains and
nishes.

oth softwoods and hardwoods may be
d for the decking surface. Western red
ar and chestnut are easy to maintain and
v to rot, but softwoods like deal and
e must be treated with preservative
ually and are prone to splintering.

ore You Start

Draw up an accurate scale plan, mark-
in any manhole covers or water pipes
incorporating any features you would
– for example, a pool, planting beds
so on.

If each square of your paper equals one
of your paving material you will find it
er to plan and order the right amount of
erials accurately. Different colours are
ul for working out more detailed pat-
s and designs.

Make sure you have all the tools and
erials you need before you start work,
do not attempt to lay paving in frosty
ther.

Mark out the site with pegs and string
g a datum peg – the peg to which all the
r pegs will refer – and use a spirit level
a straight-edge to check each peg.
ust the pegs to allow for a slight fall
ards the house – as an example, for a
around 10ft (3m) deep, you need a fall
ound 1 in 100.

Remove all the topsoil, leaving the area
hly level. The finished level must not
ss than 6in (15cm) below the building's
p-proof course. If the course is near the
nd you may have to insert a plank

*Paving and walling materials come in a
wide range of colours and finishes. These
fake stone slabs imitate riven weathered
York stone and have been co-ordinated
with imitation stone walling bricks.*

about ⅞in (2cm) thick on edge on the
footings after excavation. This will leave a
1in (2.5cm) wide gutter which can be
cleaned of any debris which might breach
the damp-proofing.

● If you are laying a hard paving material,
a 3in (7.5cm) layer of hardcore (broken
stones, brick and rubble) must be tamped
down on to the excavated soil. A heavy-
duty roller or vibrating machine can be
hired for this job.

● A 1in (2.5cm) layer of sand or sand and
cement should be put over the top of the
hardcore, raked level and then the surface
should be rolled again.

(a) Marking out the site with pegs and string is your first step.

(b) When the site is levelled, some form of edging must be laid, whether using edging blocks or timber planking.

(c) The concrete is poured on to the area then spread more evenly with a shovel before levelling using a length of timber.

(d) The concrete is levelled before the slabs are laid.

(e) Stack your slabs close at hand when paving. Having to travel some distance to fetch each one will make a long job of it.

(a)

(f) Laying the second row of complete pavers.

(g) Two rows laid. A plank helps keep feet off the wet cement. It is essential that the paving is kept level. It must be checked at every stage.

(h) A couple of short pieces of timber make handy spacers if you want a regular gap between pavers.

(i) Lay all the complete slabs first, checking after each one that it is level and that you are following your pattern plan correctly.

(d)

(j) When all the complete slabs are laid, lay the cut ones. Here, a slab is marked for cutting.

(g)

(h)

(c)

(f)

(j)

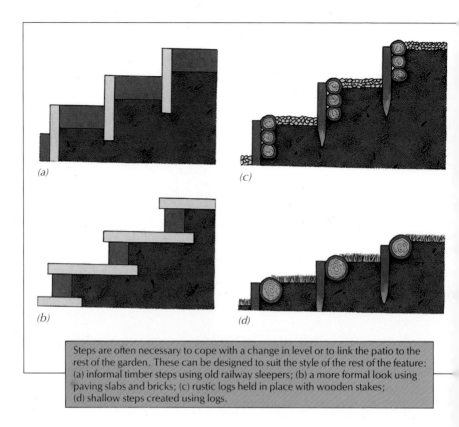

(a)

(b)

(c)

(d)

Steps are often necessary to cope with a change in level or to link the patio to the rest of the garden. These can be designed to suit the style of the rest of the feature: (a) informal timber steps using old railway sleepers; (b) a more formal look using paving slabs and bricks; (c) rustic logs held in place with wooden stakes; (d) shallow steps created using logs.

Laying Concrete

Concrete is mixed from cement, sand (usually clean river sand or sharp sand), an aggregate of pebbles or shingle, and water. You will need to calculate for a thickness of around 3in (7.5cm), and should use a ratio of one part cement to two parts sand and three parts aggregate. To calculate how much cement you need, measure the total area and multiply it by the depth – 3in (7.5cm). To this cubic measurement, add about ten per cent for wastage.

A cement mixer is recommended for larger areas as mixing by hand can be a long and tedious job. Mixers can be hired if you do not have one of your own, and are either electrically powered or petrol dr The concrete needs to be mixed until an even consistency and texture; add enough water to bind the other together into a stiff paste. If it is mor mud, add more dry ingredients. A buck barrow can be used to measure the accurately. There are various product can add to improve the concrete's resistance, to render it waterproof colour it.

When the area has been prepare described, set in an edge of brick, timl kerbstones according to preference, m sure that they are straight and level. If is to be no formal edging, a temp framework of wooden shuttering will

e erected. When this has been done the
crete can be poured over the area – aim
as continuous and even a motion as
ible. The surface should be smoothed
a plank after laying. A finer finish can
chieved by tamping the board towards
edging in a continuous chopping
ion. It is important not to overdo this
e, as if you do so the cement will begin
eaken. The surface can be smoothed to
ne finish with a float after about four
rs; if you prefer a slightly rougher, more
ured finish brush it with a soft broom.
there is any risk of rain or frost before
concrete has hardened, you should
er the area with polythene or a tarpaulin
otect it.

ing Paving Slabs

:op of the prepared sand (*see* page 17),
about 1in (2.5cm) of mortar on which
will position the slabs. The mortar must
evelled with a screed board and gently
pressed. Alternatively, dot bedding
tar on the back of each slab – a dab on
n corner and one in the centre. As every
is positioned, it must be tapped down
ly using a piece of timber to soften the
v and to prevent it cracking. The slab
uld be firm and stable with no tendency
t or rock. A straight-edge is needed to
:k that each slab is level with its neigh-
rs. An uneven patio is not only poten-
' dangerous and inconvenient, but will
collect puddles.
ne best plan when laying the slabs is to
in one corner and to work methodi-
' until all the complete slabs are laid. It
es sense to plan the patio in such a way
no cutting is required as this can be
y and wasteful. However, this is not
ys possible and you may have to hire
e kind of cutting device such as an
e grinder. If you are laying crazy pav-
it is best to lay the outer edges first, and

Saxifrage   An ideal plant for alpine sink
gardens and patio walls, and for growing
between crazy paving; the mossy varieties
make a dense carpet of evergreen, moss-like
leaves which produce a colourful mass of tiny
flowers in spring. New plants can be
propagated by seed in autumn, but are more
easily cultivated from rooted offsets taken
from the parent plant.

then to work towards the middle to avoid an
uneven edge.
   The slabs can be butted up together, or a
gap of around ½in (1.2cm) can be left using
a piece of timber as a width gauge. The
gaps can be pointed later with smoothed
mortar or, if preferred, filled with loose
sand or soil to allow creeping plants to grow
and to soften the edges of the paving.

Constructing Timber Decking

Timber decking gives an extremely stylish

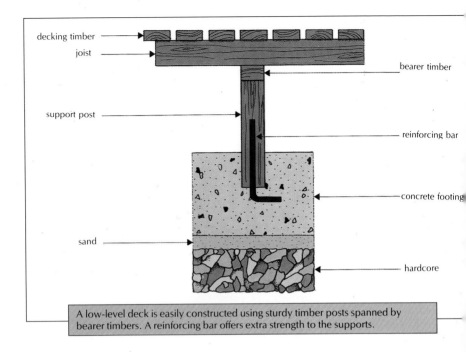

A low-level deck is easily constructed using sturdy timber posts spanned by bearer timbers. A reinforcing bar offers extra strength to the supports.

feature for minimum expertise. Unless you want it to be raised higher than 3ft (1m) off the ground, or the site is unstable or on different levels, the decking is relatively simple to install.

You can construct a low-level deck using metal fencing post spikes – these prevent the timber of the supporting posts rotting where they touch with the ground – or you could use specially treated posts. The posts should either be 4 × 4in (10 × 10cm) or 6 × 6in (15 × 15cm) depending on the distance intended between the bearing timbers. The bearing timbers themselves should be 3 × 4in (7.5 × 10cm). The surface timber may be 1 × 2in (2.5 × 5cm), 1 × 3in (2.5 × 7.5cm) or 1 × 4in (2.5 × 10cm) with a slightly bevelled edge for a fine finish.

The decking timber can be laid straight, or, if you have the confidence and the time, on the diagonal to create a zigzag pattern or even a herring-bone or basket-we design. Remember though that every t the wood changes direction it will nee be nailed to a supporting timber.

Supporting posts must be no more t 6ft (1.8m) apart and the horizontal j between them 3–4ft (1–1.2m) apart – will allow the timbers to overhang bearers by approximately 3in (7.5cm) neater, more attractive finish. It is a g idea to cut all the ends together when decking is finished to avoid a ragged e All screws and nails should be galvani and screw heads countersunk for a ne and safer finish.

Taller decks will require expert ac and will also need a handrail, but the is easily made by attaching a horizonta to extended support posts – either a le of rounded timber with a diamete around 3in (7.5cm) or a piece of bar are ideal.

• PLANTING IDEAS AND CONTAINERS

the relatively controlled environment of
patio, plants can be used to marvellous
vantage, their shape and colour cleverly
ploited to produce a balanced yet excit-
display all year round. Plants are the soft
nishings of your 'outdoor room' – creep-
can soften the paving and climbers dress
disguise walls, fences and trellises. There
built-in beds to fill with subtle colour
emes or dramatic contrasts of shape and
, and pots and tubs to provide ever-
nging focal points of seasonal interest.
When planning a scheme the first thing to
sider is whether the plants will thrive. A
py, healthy plant can only enhance
r garden, and sun/shade or soil acidity
ld make a huge difference between
ood-looking specimen and a sickly
. Providing the plants are chosen and

*Even a single plant group can offer a
wonderful variety of foliage shapes and
colours as this collection of mints reveals.
Herbs offer a medley of scents too: here,
lemon and pineapple mingle with eau de
cologne and spearmint.*

Give some thought to how pots and tubs can best be arranged. Smaller containers
such as these still have plenty of impact when grouped closely together at the foot
of a short flight of steps.

positioned with this in mind, you can con-
centrate on creating colour harmonies and
dramatic contrasts.

A basic planting scheme of a few different
and reliable evergreens ensures the patio
looks good and provides something of
interest all year round; look for contrasting
leaf shapes such as arrowheads, heart
shapes, ferny fronds or the large, pleated
cushion-like leaves of hostas. You can
either be subtle with your colour combina-
tions – and remember, leaves offer a wonderfully wide spectrum of colours too – or
dazzle the eyes with a blazing display of
bright, clashing blooms. A single or two-
colour scheme such as green and white can
be remarkably effective and works particularly well in a small environment where it
seems to create the impression of space.

Plan for seasonal interest too: spring
flowers among the more sombre evergreens
of winter; the glorious annuals of summer
followed by a few late-blooming or berried
plants – usually in tones of russet or gold –
before winter. Even in the darkest months
there is still the chance to grow a few

berried shrubs, bright pansies or swe
scented winter jasmine along your trellis
you are unsure of your plant planning sk
plot it all out on paper first using colou
pencils if you want to see the kind of ef
you might achieve; tracing paper over
are useful for showing seasonal highlig
It need not require a high level of art
skill – just a rough idea of size and co
will give you an idea of what you
achieve. You should also not forget to
for a good variety of heights and width
well as shapes and colours.

Patio Beds

Permanent planting beds within your p
scheme will not only create a more inte
ing and varied layout, they will also
the opportunity to grow a wider variet
plants. Virtually anything can be grow
container – even trees and shrubs, altho
these will require extra care and t
growth will be stunted if their roots
restricted in this way. A permanent be
also useful for growing any climbers
hope to train up a trellis, wall or perg
You can leave gaps in your paving as p
ing spaces which can be a convenient
to break up the monotony of a large are
simply used to introduce a softer elen
into the scheme. Here the shape and si:
the beds will be determined to some e>
by that of your paving.

Raised beds are a popular and
stronger element within the patio de
Usually constructed in a matching mat
the beds might be free standing or
against the back wall, and built from b
stone, timber or ornamental concrete
ing blocks. They can be any shape or
you choose, from squares and rectangi
circular or irregularly curved beds. R
beds can also look stunning when gec
ric forms interlock and incorporate bu
seating and other features. Ideally,

*Bright free-flowering Busy Lizzie are
perfect for patio pots and baskets.*

ating a raised bed using paving slabs. The soil is dug out to a depth of about 12in (30cm) and
the slab is placed in position against the paved surface, checking that it is upright and
. Hardcore is piled behind to hold it in place. When all the slabs are in position, the layer
ardcore is built up to 12in (30cm), and then topped with a layer of gravel or pebbles before
ly filling with compost.

th of soil should be around 18–24in
-60cm) and drainage holes should be
rporated in the sides of the retaining
at ground level. If you are worried
ut the paving becoming stained from
overflow, you could always incorpor-
a gulley when constructing the main
o to take the dirty water conveniently to
nearest drain.

ll the beds with a good layer of rubble
hingle for drainage, then top with a free-
ning compost or topsoil. One of the
antages of raised beds – as with contain-
- is that you can control the soil condi-
s by providing an acidic soil for lime-
rs or a chalky one for plants that prefer
line conditions.

anting areas can also be incorporated
any low walls which may divide the

*An informal raised bed filled with different
varieties of mint makes a sweet-scented
talking point on the patio.*

Baskets can be mounted on walls – useful for windy situations.

terrace or patio from the rest of the garden. Build a double wall about 2–2½ft (60–75cm) wide, filling the space between with a layer of rubble for drainage and topping this off with soil. The wall might be constructed from brick, stone or ornamental walling blocks, bedded in with mortar. Alternatively, a drystone-wall is in keeping in a rustic setting and plants can be grown in the crevices as well as along the top.

Floor to Ceiling Planting

Planting beds and free-standing containers (*see* pages 28–37) can be used to create a fine display of blooms and foliage that is instantly eye-catching. However, even with a variety of heights and sizes, the display tends to be much the same level. A more three-dimensional, attractive effect can be planned by including a few climbers, trailers and twiners for height, along with some low-growing creeping plants to soften ground area with their miniature leaves flowers. You can add height to your sche in many ways, and this can also be us for creating some shelter or privacy. might wish to clothe or disguise a fer wall or trellis, or create a special fea with an archway, a pergola or with standing screens.

There are many beautiful plants that make a splendid curtain effect, and choice will depend on when you want th to look their best and on which are own personal favourites. Ivies are obvious choice for evergreen cover – do forget that there are a great many hyb which include golden varieties and th with interesting leaf shapes. But perf you would prefer a fast-growing everg honeysuckle which has the bonus of sw smelling flowers, or an evergreen clem Clematis is perhaps one of the most pop climbing plants; there is a huge variet rids which flower at different times of year and which make a wonderful 'lay for patios.

here are climbers for every situation and every time of the year – what could be 'e lovely than the poignant scent of a ter-flowering jasmine? A sheltered wall rellis may open the scope wider to a ice of tender plants like the spectacular sion flower *Passiflora*, the beautiful gainvillaea so reminiscent of the Medi- nean or the fruiting kiwi fruit, *Actinidia* iensis.

you feel the need for something of rest at ground level, you could leave II planting spaces between your paving escribed on page 21, but instead of

Roses With their superb deep velvet colours and sweet scent, roses make a beautiful permanent feature on the patio. The compact bush varieties do particularly well in containers and raised beds if well fed and watered during the flowering season. If your patio is not really large enough for the grandeur of a hybrid tea reaching up to 30in (75cm), why not plant a *Rosa floribunda* or cluster-flowered bush rose, some of which grow only to around 18in (45cm) and are actually called 'patio roses' in many catalogues. There are miniature varieties for the smallest pots, wonderful ramblers and climbers for trellises or pergolas and a marvellous variety of types and colours to suit all tastes and situations, both sunny and shady if you choose wisely.

nd cover creeping plants are useful ten patio features and to help it blend he rest of the garden where an nal look is required.

planting taller shrubs, perennials and annuals, grow a carpet of low-growing creepers with coloured gravels, mosses and mat- or mound-forming plants. Many such plants are alpine species; they flourish in a well-drained stony soil and offer a

The juxtaposition of different containers is just as important as achieving a good balance of plant shapes and colours. Look for complementary shapes and colours as well as a variety of container sizes.

surprisingly varied array of colours and forms. Alternatively, you might enjoy a herbal carpet which emits a wonderfully pungent scent when crushed or trodden on: thyme is one of the favourites underfoot, as is the creeping chamomile 'Treneague' which has a scent like new-mown hay. Such plants also grow well in the cracks and joints between pavers, and if used in this way can soften and add colour to a large expanse of paving.

Containers

The beauty of containers is that they are free standing, thus making them to flexible. You can arrange a selection of in so many different ways: you can mix match them, move them around exchange and substitute them with the sons to keep your patio looking goo year round. Pots, tubs and baskets migf floor standing, arranged on shelves, tened to walls and fences or hung trellises or the walls of the adjoining h The patio would look bare and empty out them, for as well as providing a m of growing an essential variety of material, the containers themselves decorative and add another dimensic the overall display. For this reason

uld be chosen and arranged carefully for
best effect.

A group of different-sized containers in
same style — perhaps terracotta or tim-
— looks better than a motley arrange-
nt of different types. Try mixing shapes,
es and heights within a single material
a really stylish and successful look.
ups of odd numbers always seems to
k more natural than even numbers, and
ntainers always look better when posi-
ed in close groups which allow adja-
t plants to mingle, rather than if dotted
ut the area in singles.

he big advantage with containers is that
ou are not very good at visualizing your
ns, they can be moved around until you
happy with the way they look. This is
t done before they are filled with soil
l plants as the weight of filled containers
es make them a little less manoeuvrable.
ou do move them after they have been
ted, a low trolley — simply a board on
ors — will do the job easily enough. You
ht even like to change your pots around
n time to time, to create different looks
in the patio.
s most plants can be grown in contain-
the choice is unlimited. Unless you are

Shrubs and trees can make excellent patio
features if kept well fed and watered,
particularly dwarf rhododendrons and
conifers which offer such a wide variety of
shapes, styles and colours in leaf and flower.

growing a bushy shrub or a specimen tree
such as a standard orange tree or dwarf
Japanese maple (even then, a mat-forming
plant or coloured pebbles beneath looks
attractive and helps conserve moisture in

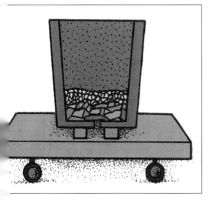

all trolley on castors is useful for
ing heavy containers into position.

The dwarf Japanese maples can make
excellent feature plants for the patio and
will grow happily in pot or tub. One of the
loveliest must be the decorative purple
Acer palmatum dissectum atropurpureum.

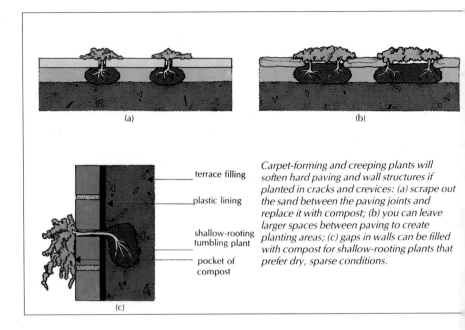

terrace filling

plastic lining

shallow-rooting
tumbling plant

pocket of
compost

Carpet-forming and creeping plants will soften hard paving and wall structures if planted in cracks and crevices: (a) scrape out the sand between the paving joints and replace it with compost; (b) you can leave larger spaces between paving to create planting areas; (c) gaps in walls can be filled with compost for shallow-rooting plants that prefer dry, sparse conditions.

the soil), plants look better if planted in groups within a single container. You can have fun choosing compatible yet complementary species to provide the effect you desire. First of all, the plants must enjoy the same kind of light and soil conditions. Then aim for a strong contrast of shape and colour, or a harmonious blend of shades. A variety of heights is important if the container is to look good as an arrangement. Taller plants should be positioned to the rear or centre of the group, with shorter plants placed to the front.

Creeping or trailing varieties are useful to train over the rim of containers and to soften their outline. For a well-balanced, mature-looking scheme it helps to have at least a few permanent plants such as evergreens, small shrubs or dwarf conifers. This will help maintain interest in winter when other plants have died back. Add seasonal specials (these can be changed every year to maintain variety and interest), spring bulbs,

summer annuals and other bedd
varieties. You can have fun planning di
ent colour harmonies and dramatic contrasts, and can either grow your c
from seed or buy them as young pla
Containers can also be prepared in adva
and then positioned on the patio as
reach their peak if you prefer the are
look in top condition all the time.

Pots of Style

Clay pots are instantly appealing with
reassuringly familiar shape and warm r
colour; they often look as good empt
they do filled with plants. There is a
range of sizes available, from the tiny
(50mm) diameter pot up to giant vers
big enough to plant a small tree and w
diameter of 18–24in (45–60cm). Howe
sizes smaller than 6in (15cm) are only r
suitable for propagating seedlings
plantlets, and not for display purposes.

also buy half-pots (about half the height
tandard pots) for low-growing plants,
clay pans which are about a third of the
of standard pots and which are useful
lpine displays.

ts can be plain, patterned or highly
orative, fat bellied, with or without
s' or handles, or garnished with relief
oration of fruit, flowers and cherubs.
y are made in imitation of traditional
s such as Venetian, Tuscan or Minoan.
y seem to suit virtually any type of
me, but are particularly effective when

*Old chimney pots make good patio plant
containers and provide a bit of height.*

dodendrons and azaleas   The dwarf
ns are ideal for growing in large containers
he patio, and for creating a more mature,
blished look. In fact, if your garden has
ky soil this is the only way you will be
to enjoy this spectacular group of
ering shrubs as they are lime-haters.
tainers can be filled with a good acid
post and should be kept well watered but
waterlogged. The tiny Japanese azaleas
v to only 20–30in (50–75cm) and most
evergreen; the deciduous azaleas might
h 5ft (1.5m), but they are hardy and
luce some spectacular blooms. There is
qually wide choice among the dwarf
lodendrons, these growing to anything
veen 6–35in (15–90cm), including the
pact, free-flowering *Rhododendron
simanum* hybrids.

planning a Mediterranean theme or a herb
garden. Their biggest drawback is that they
are very porous which means the soil dries
out quickly – this is perhaps the reason why
they are especially suited to plants which
prefer a fast-draining soil. To reduce the
burden of watering frequently, you could
mulch the surface of the compost with bark,
fibre or small pebbles to minimize moisture
loss. Alternatively, you could turn the pot's
natural porosity to your advantage by standing it on a matching saucer of water which
it will absorb gradually. This also prevents
ugly water spills on your paving.

Another disadvantage of terracotta containers is that they chip easily and are prone
to frost damage – this is especially true of
the ornamental pots, although even the
frost-resistant types will be damaged by
extremely cold conditions. They can be
wrapped in hessian sacking for the winter,
but this is not really practical if they are still
on show. After a while, clay pots will also

Wall-mounted baskets can add extra interest at eye-level.

thus keeping the main display in peak condition. Plastic pots come in a choice terracotta, white, black or green and easily cracked or broken. They are also light, making them unsuitable for large plants which are likely to blow over although there is a range of heavier, better quality plastic pots available.

A classically styled urn filled with attractive foliage plants.

develop a kind of green bloom due to moss growth, but many gardeners quite like this effect and are happy to leave such pots uncleaned. Similar style pots which lack the high porosity and frost-tender problems are available in stone – more usually reconstituted stone these days – and these look good in a mellow or rustic scheme.

You can also buy a similar range of plain sizes and styles in plastic which have the advantages of being inexpensive and offering good moisture retention, thus making them suitable for plants which prefer a damp soil. However, such pots are not particularly attractive and are more usually used as liners inside more ornamental containers. Using them in this way offers the advantage of planting up and substituting a new liner as the old plant starts to die back,

Urns, Jars and Bowls

Large urns and jars for the patio are usually made of terracotta, although these sometimes glazed and decorated with or classical motifs. Being narrow need they are not suitable for most plants, but look good as part of an arrangement similar pots, or when positioned on a wall or shelf as a patio ornament. bowls are also becoming increasingly popular for displaying a collection of sea

*...orative urns make splendid patio
...ments.*

...ts of a similar height – for example,
...ng blooms or summer bedding. This
...duces the required massed effect. Made
...rracotta, stone or concrete, these large
...ls can be mounted on special supports
...ositioned on a wall or table.

...s, Boxes and Barrels

...oden tubs are ideal for a hot, sunny
...tion as they hold moisture well. They
...e in a wide range of sizes, the larger
...s being particularly suitable for large
...nanent plants such as shrubs, trees and
...bers, or for massed arrangements of

many plants. If stained or painted they can
look very smart and will suit both a formal
or rustic patio, being the perfect match for
other timber features such as pergolas, trellises or patio furniture. A less expensive
option is to buy cut-down barrels – these
have a more 'countrified' appearance. Full-
size barrels can also have their uses, with
2in (5cm) holes drilled 8in (20cm) apart for
inserting strawberry plants, cherry tomatoes
or herbs – an excellent way to grow a large
number of productive plants in the minimum of patio space. You can also buy
specially made PVC or terracotta planters
designed for herbs or strawberries.

More ornamental are the traditional Versailles planters constructed from timber
slats, and sometimes featuring a slide-out
section which is useful for removing the
plants, replacing compost and so on. These
may feature a natural stain or varnish, or be

*Timber planters come in many shapes and
styles and have a pleasant warm
appearance that suits informal plant groups.*

painted white or even a pastel shade for a more modern patio scheme. Many such planters feature decorative finials at the four corners, or pyramidal plant supports for a taller, unusual display. Versailles planters are ideal for more formal patios and ornamental plants such as standard specimen trees or topiary arrangements. They are also available in fibreglass.

Troughs and Window-Boxes

Made from timber, stone, fibreglass or concrete, long, rectangular planting troughs are useful for adding a different dimension to your patio arrangement. They can be quite ornamental and look good along a low wall if free standing on matching legs or supports. You can use them as boundary markers between patio and garden, or against a wall or fence. Some troughs and boxes are designed to fasten directly to a wall or windowsill, although they can be fixed ⬛ fence or trellis if it is strong enough to t⬛ the weight.

Window-boxes are useful for dressing⬛ a blank expanse of wall facing the pa⬛ They are usually made of wood, but ⬛ also be found in plastic or even terracotta⬛

Planters

If you are looking for simple container⬛ show off a fine collection of plants, you⬛ buy fibreglass or concrete planters wh⬛ style may be plain, but whose range⬛ heights, shapes and sizes is flexible eno⬛ to create exciting planting combinatio⬛ Available in many geometric shapes, so⬛ of which are interlocking, they look g⬛ when grouped together and each is idea⬛ planting several complementary or c⬛ trasting plants. You can use the larger s⬛ as portable raised beds.

If plants are placed in troughs and window-boxes in their pots, they are easily replaced as the flowers fade. Stand on a layer of pebbles for drainage and pack between the pots with a good moisture-retaining compost to reduce water loss.

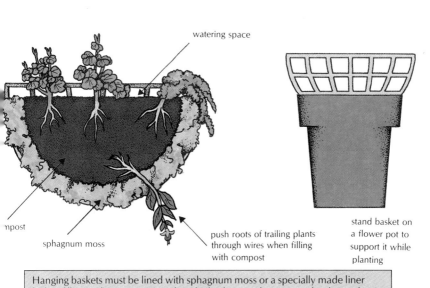

watering space

~npost

sphagnum moss

push roots of trailing plants through wires when filling with compost

stand basket on a flower pot to support it while planting

Hanging baskets must be lined with sphagnum moss or a specially made liner before filling with compost. Standing the basket on a large pot or bucket makes it easier to plant up.

)art from being relatively inexpensive – ~nportant consideration if you are look- ɔr large containers – another advantage ~t the planters are easy to scrub and ~nt if they start to look a little dirty. ·ers benefit from being raised a few ·s off the ground to aid drainage, and ·event the build-up of dirt and algae ~h contact with the ground encourages.

~ing Baskets

~ing baskets are another useful way to ~height to your planting scheme or to ~ little interest to a blank wall or other vertical feature – for example, they ɔe hung from a pergola or post. The ·t is traditionally made from galva- ~ wire (most likely to be plastic coated ~ days), but can also be solid plastic ~an integral drip-tray. The basket hangs ~ a chain or plastic hanger, and if well

planted becomes invisible beneath a three-dimensional ball of foliage and flowers.

Baskets need frequent watering as they dry out quickly, although some have water reservoirs. Sizes can vary from a diameter of approximately 12–18in (30–45cm) to ones which are as small as 8in (20cm) in diameter. Depth might be from 6–9in (15–

Hanging baskets can look good when hung from a pergola structure and are an ideal way to add interest before climbers have grown.

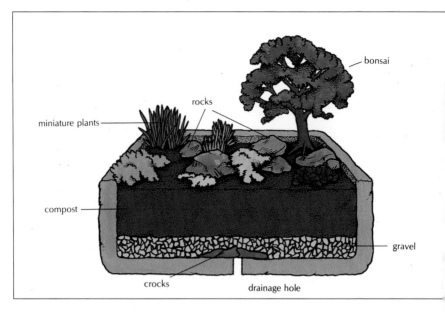

A miniature sink or trough garden.

Labels: bonsai, rocks, miniature plants, compost, gravel, crocks, drainage hole

23cm). They are usually lined with sphagnum moss or a special liner before filling. Once loaded with plants and compost, the baskets are heavy so fixings should be checked for safety. Similar baskets are also available for fixing to walls or fences.

Old sinks or stone troughs make attractive patio containers for alpine collections and seasonal plants.

Sinks and Mini-Gardens

The old traditional glazed sinks ma~ lovely feature on a cottage-style or ~ tional patio. It also does not matter if ~ are cracked or chipped when placed i~ garden. If you do not like the shiny ~ glaze, then this can be concealed bene~ layer of hypertufa (two parts spha~ peat, one part sand and one part cer~ Before applying the hypertufa, first pai~ outer sides and down to a couple of ir~ inside with a waterproof bonding a~ Mixed with water and spread about ~ (1cm) thick, the hypertufa will cre~ rough textured surface which is ver~ that of natural stone. It will finally h~ after around two weeks.

You can also buy ready-made ~ garden troughs and trays in a varie~ square and rectangular sizes with a s~ finish. The sink or trough should be ~ with a good layer of crocks or grav~

An old stone sink is perfect for a collection of alpines.

inage, before topping with a suitable ipost and planting a collection of alpines imilar small plants.

owbags

wbags are a wonderful way to convert a ier of the patio into a miniature veget-: garden, but as they do not look parti-rly attractive, stand them on specially gned trays (which prevent the paving ig marked) or drop them into custom-le frames of brick or timber. These large 'thene bags of rich, soil-less compost isure around 4ft (1.2m) long and are ect for growing tomatoes, aubergines, 'gettes and sweet peppers – in fact, hing edible that might thrive in the tered conditions of a patio. Standards ' from make to make, so do not simply the cheapest brand 'though drainage holes are made in the om of some brands of growbag, the post does not dry out as quickly as in r types of container so you do have e careful not to overwater. You should however, ever allow the compost to pletely dry out.

Tomatoes Look out for new tomato varieties which have a shorter, bushier habit – perfect for growbags and pots – or tiny cherry tomato types that can be grown in pots or hanging baskets. There is even a variety developed with hanging baskets in mind – 'Tomato Tumbler' (above) – which produces a mass of small but sweet tomatoes within a decorative ball of foliage. However, for successful results you must be prepared to feed and water tomato plants in pots and hanging baskets regularly as their exposed position will cause them to dry out more quickly.

Tall crops such as tomatoes will need staking, the most secure method being a plastic-coated steel frame which fits neatly around the bag. Canes are not really practical as there is not sufficient depth of compost to keep them from toppling over, but a system of strings can be effective if the bag is positioned against a wall. The bags will also need feeding regularly if fruiting plants are to crop well.

4 • DECORATION AND FURNITURE

A well-planned layout, interesting paving and an exciting blend of plants will create an attractive patio, but it is those finishing touches and final furnishings which make your 'outdoor room' really special. The area may need some kind of focal point such as a statue or free-standing fountain, or perhaps a dull corner or blank wall will need something of interest to brighten it up or to distract attention away from it.

There is a wide range of garden ornaments and outdoor statuary available, and just a couple of well-chosen items could give your scheme exactly the feel or effect you need. You might wish to capture an oriental look with a stone buddha or bamboo stand among sand, gravel and lots of architectural greenery. Or perhaps a bright umbrella and a few large white stones are all that is needed to transform your terracotta pots of herbs and bright flowers into a Mediterranean-style retreat.

Position is as important as choice. A large item might be set off by a formal alcove, stone or trellis-work, or by a dark backdrop of greenery. Smaller objects may need a plinth, table or shelf to bring them into prominence. A matching pair of ornaments can look very effective when flanking an opening in a patio wall or on either side of steps leading down into the garden.

Garden centres and garden shops stock a wide range of tempting outdoor *objets d'art* in stone, terracotta, pottery, metal and even wickerwork, from figures and animals to interpretations of floral and fruit themes. You might even be lucky enough to find antique garden ornaments in metal, stone or lead at shops and auctions. If your budget is tight there are plenty of 'junk' objects that make interesting patio ornaments – for example, an interesting rock, a piece of driftwood, old weathered basket or a wooden cartwheel. Experiment with mirrors which are a great idea for small patios where they can be placed

In the right setting, a few carefully chosen accessories will create an oriental atmosphere.

There is a wide range of small garden ornaments to choose from, including stone animals which are useful for tucking into corners or arranging on shelves. Plants can also be ornamental like these closely clipped evergreens which have been trained into geometric shapes, or an arrangement of bold architectural species.

...iring only annual maintenance, ...den bench seats and chairs can look ...all year round, especially when they ...s decoratively crafted as these.

strategically to effectively double its size. Or if faced with a large blank wall, why not disguise it behind a *trompe l'oeil* painting of a splendid garden or a realistic looking landscape?

Somewhere to sit

Since a patio is essentially designed as a pleasant place to sit outdoors, your choice of furniture must be of prime importance. The choice of styles is vast, from permanent benches which are not especially comfortable but which can be left in position all year round to provide somewhere to sit for five minutes' enjoyment of the morning paper, to elegant outdoor dining furniture

An elegant bamboo lounger adds an air of sophistication to the patio, yet folds away for easy storage. A simple but very effective group of plants instantly reinforces the right kind of atmosphere.

It is worth looking out for furniture that can be collapsed or folded away for easy storage at the end of the season.

and plushly upholstered loungers w have to be brought indoors at the er each day. Your choice will be influence how you use your patio – is it a plac relaxation, for dining or entertaining, combination of these roles? You must consider how much space you hav some patio furniture ranges are quite b As some types have to be put under co night or stored away at the end of sum you will have to decide if you have space to store them in your garage, she outbuilding. Furniture which folds aw worth considering where indoor spa limited.

The simple garden bench seat is us made of timber. It can be as plain as a bench or more ornamental in imitatic

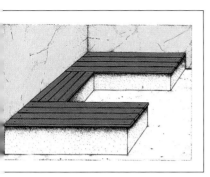

*'lt-in bench-type seating for the fully
'grated patio.*

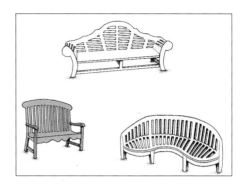

*Stylish ornamental garden seats in a
classic style.*

'yens' attractive latticed-back seat – per-
t when set against a backdrop of ever-
ens. Decorative cast-metal seats in rep-
luction Victorian styles are also available
a permanent position on the patio. For a
r-round dining area, timber and metal
r the best choices again – wooden
nic bench tables are simple to construct
h a minimum of carpentry knowledge.
ber chairs and tables come in a wide
ice of sizes and styles, some of which
extremely elegant considering they are
garden use, and you can have them

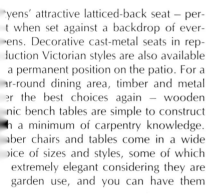

*nber bench, a patio table and a simple
ic bench with built-in seating.*

finished in any one of many different stains
and colours. The old-fashioned cast-metal
chairs and tables are also ideal for patios,
especially where space is limited as a circular table and a couple of chairs seem to take
up virtually no room at all.

Moulded plastic styles can be equally
stylish these days and are quite durable.
The better quality patio sets can look very
smart if the patio has a distinct Mediterranean atmosphere, or if arranged on a pool-
side paved area. Many are available with
sun-proof upholstery for real garden comfort. These cushions can usually be
removed for cleaning and winter storage. If
you simply want something lightweight but
comfortable, folding metal-frame chairs can
be stacked, and the covers are easily replaced when they begin to wear.

For lounging, again there is a wide
choice, but for comfort and economy you
cannot beat the traditional deckchair – it is
simple, it stores flat and it is easily reno-
vated with a lick of paint and a new length
of bright canvas material, available from
good haberdashery shops. Most loungers
are designed to fold away. There are
the elegant colonial-style wooden or rattan
chairs, minimalist plastic scoops for
dedicated sun-worshippers and the ultimate
in comfort – thickly padded loungers

Stylish furniture and ornaments can transform the humblest patio into a delightful outdoor living area.

Upholstered patio furniture combines good looks and comfort.

cushions, a drinks trolley, cloths, cut[l]
and china — these can also all be [co-]
ordinated. There are even special ran[ge]
you can buy which are suited to outd[oor]
use. A cupboard in the summer-house [or]
shed is useful for storing such garden-c[are]
items and keeps them out of the house.

complete with elbow rests, reclining foot-
and head-pads, integral shelves and a
matching bar trolley.

Of course, you do not have to buy a
matching set of furniture for the patio.
Improvising can be fun, and such an
arrangement could look less contrived in a
rustic or informal-style setting. Range folding or old wickerwork chairs around a
wooden table, or create a simple bench seat
with a large plank and a couple of sawn-off
stumps. An old marble-topped wash-stand
might make a good garden table, or an old
wrought-iron trestle sewing machine with a
new top will make a good table.

There are lots of other patio furnishings
and accessories you can have fun choosing
and which are mostly brought in at the end
of the day: patio umbrellas for extra shade
over the dining area, comfortable rugs and

Stone furniture can be left outdoors on the patio all year round, although an umbrella is a useful summer addition.

er Dark

with any room indoors, good lighting is
ential on the patio, this being particu-
ly true of the patio whose use can be
ended three-fold by the simple installa-
of a few subtle lighting effects. As well
highlighting one of your best features
n the house, you will actually be able to
out there and enjoy it on fine evenings,
ether simply to sit and relax among the
dy scent of the plants, or to enjoy a meal
a party with friends. Good lighting can
be an important security factor for
erring intruders.

door lamps and lanterns not only
le the patio area to be used after dark,
an also produce wonderful effects to
njoyed from house or garden.

you can plan your lighting scheme at
initial design stages of your patio, so
h the better. This way all the wiring and
e of the fitments can be concealed;
the lights can be chosen to comple-
t your proposed patio features. Exterior
es must be protected by a special plas-
conduit and buried to a depth of at

An art deco patio gas lamp – a real
treasure and only one of many antique
garden features that could grace your
patio.

least 18in (46cm). If this is not possible
because the patio has already been constructed, it is sometimes possible to peg the
wires safely along the top of a wall or fence
with special fixing clips, or to recess it into
the mortar pointing of a wall. Unless you
have previous experience, it is best to have
such outdoor lighting installed by a qual-
ified electrician. Fitments used should be
recommended specifically for outdoor use,
and the system fitted with an RCB (residual
circuit breaker) which will cut off the power
immediately there is any deviation in the
current.

Garden light fittings vary from between
150W and 300W. As there is a limit to the

number of lights you will be able to run from a single cable, you may have to plan for two or three such cables or a single thicker one. The distance the cable runs from the mains will also affect its capacity as levels can drop significantly – this is an important consideration if you would like to extend your lighting scheme to the rest of the garden, or along paths and drives. Another feature which causes a drain on power, and one which you may not have thought of, is a water pump which runs moving water features such as cascades and fountains.

There are many lighting effects you can experiment with outdoors. Ideally, you should aim at a combination of several of these which can be operated independently; this looks far more subtle than one blaze of light. There are three basic types of light, each of which creates a different kind of effect: tungsten produces a warm yellow light; low-voltage halogen bulbs are clear and white; and discharge lighting gives a colder blue-green tinge.

Fitments include uplighters, downlighters and spotlights. Some spotlights incorporate a spike which allows them to be inserted securely in tubs or planting beds, the light filtering interestingly through the foliage. Downlighters fitted to pergolas, walls and fences are useful to highlight plants and features, and also to cast a decent light over the barbecue or dining table. Again, filtering the light through the leaves of a tree will help avoid any glare. Floodlights produce more of a general wash of light rather than a directional one, and can be particularly effective washing the wall of a building and highlighting any interesting architectural features. Well lights also make useful uplighters; these are sunk into the ground and lie concealed behind toughened safety glass or a special grid.

There are also low-voltage underwater lights which can be used to make a night-time feature of fountains and pools. Some

Petunias   These versatile plants make a wonderfully bright patio bloom. They thrive in a sunny, sheltered position, producing an eye-catching display of colour and pattern i hanging baskets, window-boxes and patio tubs. The large trumpet-like blooms in brilliant shades of shocking pink, purple and mauve may be strikingly marked with white or black, and while the flowers can be spoi by rain, regular deadheading ensures a long flowering season. The newest hybrids offer beautifully frilled double forms and a compact, bushy plant that is ideal for tubs a containers.

are coloured red, blue or green, but white or blue lights are generally k Alternatively, you could make the mo water's reflective benefits by highligh plants and features around a pool catching their reflection in the pool. C lights are designed to be seen as well highlight the patio; outdoor bulkhead l can be fixed to walls for a good non-g light. Floor-standing and wall-mou ornamental lanterns can also be use decorative accessories, and can be par larly effective when placed on either si an entrance or patio steps. Other lamp specially designed to flank steps or path

For special occasions, the soft flick light of candles or night-lights strung ir jars transforms the patio into a rom setting, and some candles will even insects. Tiny fairy lights can also be s around pergolas, along walls and in for parties.

• WATER ON THE PATIO

pool or fountain may not be an obvious
oice for a patio feature, but in fact will
ke an excellent focal point even if you
ly install something as small as a simple
ter spout spilling into a bowl. Water is
becially suited to small places, as its
lecting qualities and sparkle seem to
d light and movement. Then there is the
axing sound of moving water and the sight
light playing on the water, with maybe a
 fish swimming and the ever-changing

*A free-standing water fountain utilizing an
old stone millwheel makes a delightful
moving water feature in the minimum
of space.*

ters   Many of the old traditional border
rennials have been adapted for use as
ourful bedding plants, producing faster
wing and compact plants with plenty of
ooms. The dwarf asters are worth growing
 their colourful mass of blue, pink, red and
ite flowers in star-like, globular and
uble forms according to type. Being free-
wering, the blooms will smother the 6–
n (15–25cm) tall plants, making them
al for patio containers. Some of the new
arf varieties are also especially resistant to
er wilt.

reflection of clouds going by – all perfect
antidotes to today's stressful lifestyle. A
formal style water feature is also well suited
to integrating into a patio plan.

A pool can be sunken or raised with
matching paved materials. A bubble fountain or spout can easily be fitted into a
paving space or patio wall. It makes sense
to decide on such a feature at the early
planning stages of your patio so that it can
be fully integrated with other features such
as built-in seating and raised beds.
However, if the patio is already established,
you could always install a raised pool or
moving water feature – some of these have
even been designed to fit into a patio pot or
plant tub.

Patio Pools

If you love the idea of water in the garden,
your patio pool could almost take up the
larger part of the patio area, with timber

A wall-mounted spout and a brick-faced corner pool make a delightful feature for the tiniest sized patio.

Containers sunk into the ground and surrounded by timber or pebbles are a simple but effective way to create a pool on the patio.

decks around it for seating and eating. This will give the impression that the patio is much larger than it really is, and it will also be cheaper on paving. Alternatively, even the smallest pool with a miniature water lily and a few fish will offer hours of pleasure for the minimum of space.

Sunken Pools

A sunken pool can be any shape and style, from an informal curve with more of a wildlife feel to it, to a strict geometric shape echoing the style of your paving and other hard landscaping features.

It can be constructed in one of several ways. First, dig your hole, checking at every stage that it is level with a straight-edge and spirit level. A narrow shelf about 10–12in (25–30cm) below the top level is useful for standing marginal plants. Pre-moulded semi-rigid pools are available in a variety of shapes and sizes, and made from either fibreglass or plastic. A hole must be dug to the correct size with as few gaps around the liner as possible. A lining of sand helps it fit

more snugly. Although this type limits y to a particular shape, it is tough and qu to install, and if you put it in before the of the patio area is built other features more easily be designed around it.

If you already have a clear idea of type of pool you want, the easiest metho to use a tough PVC, butyl or similar rub lining. The lining material is bought by metre in a variety of thicknesses, and more expensive it is the better resistanc tends to have to to sunlight, frost and punc ing. To calculate how much liner you ne measure twice the depth of your excava plus its length and then add 2ft (60cm). width required will be twice the depth the width plus the 2ft (60cm). Once have checked that any sharp objects h been removed from the hole, you put 3in (7cm) layer of sand and place the over it, securing it around the sides bricks or boulders. Fill the pool wit hosepipe, and as you do so the weigl the water will pull the liner into plac can then be hidden under your pavin edging material.

Alternatively, pools can be lined concrete which, with frostproofing waterproofing additives, can be a st

long-lasting lining material. Concrete
·ld be particularly useful in a situation
·re the pool is at risk of being punctured,
·· as if it is to be used as a children's
·dling pool. However, concrete is not
· to handle if you have not worked with
·efore. Measurements and application
·t be accurate for success. The base and
·s of the pool must be at least 6in (15cm)
·k, and you will have to allow for this
·n excavating the hole.
·· estimate how much concrete you need,
· up the total area of the base and sides,
· then multiply this area by the thickness
·e concrete. The thickness of the base
· have to be subtracted from the height
·e walls, and similarly the thickness of

Hostas   Sometimes called plantain lilies,
hostas are a garden designer's affirmed
favourite. Although the plant produces spikes
of soft flowers, it is primarily grown for its
foliage which is large and thick with deep
markings like quilting. Hostas come in an
interesting range of designer colours from
blue and green to yellow or white stripes. The
plants can look good alone or in a grouped
arrangement of contrasting shapes, but they
do need to be kept well watered and free from
slugs and snails. They grow to 6–24in (15–
60cm) according to which variety you choose
to grow.

the two walls must be subtracted from the
length of the two walls opposite. You will
need a concrete mix of two parts cement to
three parts coarse aggregate and one part
sand. You can measure these accurately
using a bucket or a wheelbarrow, depending on the size of your pool.

 To reinforce the concrete, metal rods or
chicken wire are laid around the base and
up the sides; if creating a formal shape,
timber shuttering will also be required to
keep the sides straight. Rubbing the boards
with a soapy cloth prevents the concrete
sticking to the boards, and these should
simply be lifted out after the concrete has
dried. The concrete ought to be poured in a

·eometric pools edged in brick make
·active patio feature with plants
·ed to pots for easy maintenance.

A raised pool makes a delightful feature within a formal patio layout. If you calculate size and shape to use only complete bricks or stone, a square or rectangle such as this is relatively simple to construct.

single motion, making sure it is stiff enough not to sink to the bottom. Leave it to harden for at least twenty-four hours.

When the concrete is dry the pool can be filled with water, but it will be three or four days before it hardens sufficiently for it to be strong enough to stand on. In any case, a concrete-lined pool will have to be filled and emptied four or five times over a period of several weeks to reduce the toxic lime content in the cement. There is, however, a special compound you can use to seal the sides if you are impatient to get the pool stocked. Remember that you should never tackle a concreting job if the weather is likely to be frosty.

Raised Pools

Raised pools are usually formal in design, consisting of a circle, square or rectangle, or even several interlocking shapes different levels. A quick and easy opti to create a miniature pool out of a w proofed barrel or large urn. They can n a lovely feature on the patio, perhaps ir porating seating areas for observing fish plants at closer quarters, and being pe for disabled owners.

Mark out the pool in the same way a sunken one, checking that the side parallel and that it looks right in relati other structural features on the patio example, walls or fences. It will still re foundations in the form of a concrete below ground level; the mix for this w one part cement to two-and-a-half sand to five parts aggregate. You s compact this into the excavation and it. Check with pegs and string that it is before it hardens.

The pool can be faced in materi

…aterproof barrel makes an excellent …ant raised pool for the patio, with the …dition of a few miniature water plants.

water. The retaining wall must be double skinned, the space between the skins determined by the size of your proposed coping material. This wall will be built in the same way as you would tackle a patio wall (*see* pages 25–6). Build the inner wall first, but only after you have constructed at least one course of the outer wall to mark out the size and shape of the finished pool. If you cement the corners into place correctly, the rest of the course should follow true. Bricks or blocks will have to be staggered for strength, the joint in each course aligned with the centre of those above and below.

The liner is fitted in the same way as for a sunken pool, the weight of the water pulling it into position. Bricks or flat coping slabs will disguise the top of the liner and make a useful place to sit or to stand plant pots.

…ch those of the main patio, but because …he pressure of water a double liner is …t. Concrete is not really practical in this …ance as it is too prone to frost damage …ve ground. The pool is built using …cks or bricks, and it helps if you can …uce the number that need to be cut by …king the design an even number of units …en planning the pool's size and shape. … may take some adjusting with a small …l. To estimate how much material you …d, divide the length and width of the …oosed structure by the length of one of … bricks or blocks. Allow a few extra for …kages, especially if some will need …ing. Doubling the length and width will … you the number of units required for a …le course; calculate the total number of …rses by dividing the height of the …hed pond by the height of a single brick …lock.

…e liner is tucked into the top course of …ks, so this will be the final level of the

This small raised pool on the patio has everything; somewhere to sit, a bubble fountain, fish and even water lilies.

A raised circular pool is more difficult to build. You will not be able to construct a double-leaf wall as the bricks or blocks will not be properly aligned. However, laying the bricks in alternate header and stretcher courses will help to prevent them from protruding.

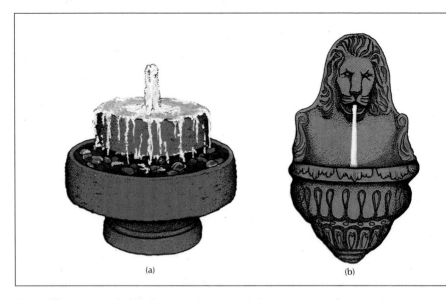

(a)

(b)

Types of fountain: (a) a bubble fountain takes up very little space on a small patio and is particularly suitable for families with young children as the water reservoir is completely concealed; (b) wall fountains can be highly ornamental and are a delightful way to incorporate running water in the minimum of space.

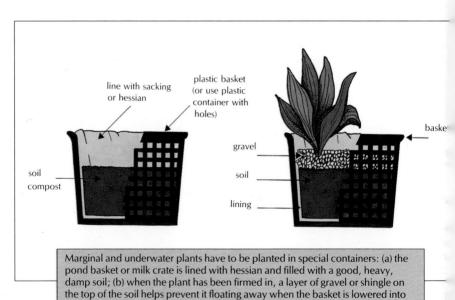

Marginal and underwater plants have to be planted in special containers: (a) the pond basket or milk crate is lined with hessian and filled with a good, heavy, damp soil; (b) when the plant has been firmed in, a layer of gravel or shingle on the top of the soil helps prevent it floating away when the basket is lowered into the water.

...e ornamental fountain can look good in a small pool and make a stunning focal point for ...n or patio.

...ing Water Features

...all pump provides the opportunity to ...e a moving water feature such as a ...rspout or cascade. As well as the ...tive sight of water falling on to stones ...o a pool, there is the relaxing sound of ...hing or trickling water to act as a ...sion. If space is really limited, the

water reservoir can be concealed – an ideal option if the patio is to be used by young children. The water falls on to a pile of pebbles or stones, these concealing a grille covering the pump and reservoir hidden underground.

Fountains come in many sizes and styles, from a simple spout to more ornamental features such as figures, fish and sculpted

A simple weir adds the formal effect of moving water and can be fully integrated into a well-planned design.

plants. Even a stone or brass ball looks attractive with water flowing over it. There can also be scope on the patio for a waterfall or cascade, and this can make a wonderful focal point. A small cascade might be used to deliver water from one pool into another on a lower level; or a formal cascade with water running over a waterproofed wall or sheet of perspex can be built as part of your patio scheme.

Where space is really tight, you might consider a wall-mounted feature like a stone mask spout. The outlet pipe can be concealed between the two courses when you construct the wall, or if the wall is already built you can sometimes remove the coping and thread the pipe through. If this is not possible, you will have to remove

some of the bricks or make a cha through the block wall using a hammer chisel, replastering the wall afterward you do not think that this will be enough, then you may have to con rebuilding a section of the wall.

A water pump can also be used to ate a stream or watercourse — a device to mark the boundary between and garden, or to act as a divider on a patio. This feature does not slope would in nature, otherwise the water rush to the bottom of the slope and w be pumped up again. The stream should be laid on the level. Creat informal look with large boulders and vegetation; or make it a strictly geon watercourse, almost like a moat.

• BARBECUES

th all the excitement of creating a com-
table and attractive outdoor living area,
not forget the outdoor kitchen – a barbe-
e. They say that food tastes better when
en outdoors; well it tastes great when
oked outdoors too. You simply cannot
at the flavour of charcoal-grilled food,
d it is not as difficult to get good results as
may seem at first to the complete barbe-
e novice – if you follow the rules you can
rantee excellent results every time.

A new patio is the ideal opportunity to
n a proper barbecue area. First,
vever, you need the right equipment,
d this will vary according to your
erience and your needs.

is a good idea to plan ahead as you may
ntually upgrade your barbecue equip-
nt to more sophisticated models as your
fidence grows.

Types of Barbecue

Your local garage and DIY store probably
sell disposable barbecues in a foil tray;
these are great for picnics, but if you like the
fun and flavour of barbecuing it is worth
having a proper barbecue on the patio.

Hibachi Grill

The smallest and simplest type is the tiny
Hibachi grill. It has a small round or square
bowl, and may be floor standing (position it
on a table or a shelf for better accessibility)
or comes with detachable legs. The Hibachi
is ideal for occasional barbecues where you
are feeding just a couple of people, and is
the best option where space is limited as
you can bring it out when you need it and
store it away easily when you do not.

(a)   (b)

The free-standing barbecue can be as simple or sophisticated as you need: (a) a
trolley gas-powered grill with temperature gauge, warming rack, lid and extra
burner; (b) a simple grill with a wind shield is adequate for just a couple of people
and folds away neatly when not in use.

A decorative, circular, built-in barbecue incorporating a useful wide, flat surface for seating and serving.

However, if you are likely to be barbecuing more often or are keen to hold barbecue parties where you will be catering for a great many people, it is time to upgrade to a more sophisticated model. It is a mistake to struggle with inadequate equipment – this is the main reason why barbecues get a bad name – and is a bit like trying to cater for a dinner party on a tiny primus stove.

Kettle Barbecues

You can buy larger machines called kettle barbecues which look like a giant hamburger bun on legs. These cannot only cope with more cooking, but also offer a draught-control system. Some are large enough to cook a whole turkey. The more you pay, the easier the machines are to use and the more they can handle; the top-of-the-range gas-fired models even do away with burning charcoal!

Gas Barbecues

Gas-powered barbecues are fuelled by tled propane gas, yet still retain that sm charcoal flavour by means of special r over which the food is cooked. Mounte a trolley, most of these offer better faci than your kitchen cooker indoors: rotisserie, corn roaster, kebab attachn and even a preparation surface, bottle and storage shelves. The machines are and heavy, so you need plenty of spa which to store them – not forgetting gas bottle.

Electric Barbecues

A few barbecues are electrically pow the obvious drawback being that you access to a power point. If you hav room, it is possible to build in these b more sophisticated machines and cre

A permanent brick or stone barbecue is easily built in using a standard kit which supplies all the necessary grids and utensils.

ecue corner or complex within your
plans, complete with sheltered seating
and table.

nanent Barbecues

do not have to have large, expensive
oment to enjoy the advantages of a
-in barbecue. A permanent structure is
/ incorporated into your patio design.
kits are readily available and include
necessary racks, charcoal grids and
olate (for collecting the ash) which fit a
-sided brick structure about 4ft (1.2m)
and waist high.
u need to use solid concrete blocks (do
se the lightweight type as they will not

be able to take the heat), ideally measuring
9 × 9 × 12in (23 × 23 × 31cm). You will
only require about eight blocks for the
simplest barbecue, along with a 2in (5cm)
thick 2 × 3ft (60 × 100cm) paving slab to
act as the hearth. This basic design can be
expanded to provide a larger complex
including a work surface and seating.

A more ambitious project would be a
circular barbecue, designed more as a focal
point, and incorporating seating and serving areas. When positioning a permanent
barbecue area you should make sure it is
well sheltered as wind makes the charcoal
flare. Do not place the barbecue too close
to trees which are likely to shed leaves and
twigs over the cooking area. Some people

A sheltered barbecue complex.

like to build a permanent chimney over the cooking area in order to reduce the amount of smoke.

The Art of Barbecuing

Cooking on a barbecue is not as difficult as some make it seem; clouds of smoke and undercooked food is not the way to do it. For a start, you should make sure that you use only good quality charcoal and the right kind of starter. You should never use methylated spirit, paraffin, petrol or wood kindling to start the fire, but should instead use a properly recommended barbecue starter which comes in paste or liquid form.

The charcoal itself also comes in two main forms: treated chips – pieces of charcoal wood which light quickly in about ten minutes without the need for a proprietary

starter; and briquettes which are hard light and need the help of a fire-light barbecue starter. The latter will take ι thirty minutes to reach the right stag cooking – that is, when there is no sι and the charcoal is glowing hot. C bags of charcoal, which are in fact ture of wood, briquettes and broken are best avoided, as are wood, house and peat, none of which will bart successfully.

When the fire is ready, sprinkle it v few aromatic herbs, then oil the gι prevent the food from sticking. Of cc things are a lot easier and quicker w power-assisted barbecue: you simply ι on, ignite it, adjust the temperature away you go.

It is best to marinate food which intend to cook on the barbecue as th tenderize the meat as well as steepι

wour. Brush the food with melted butter
· vegetable oil before cooking and do not
it too much on the grill at any one time as
o much fat dripping on to the coals will
use them to smoke.

Some barbecues offer the option of
osed cooking, and these operate more
e a conventional oven. You can cook
hole joints, or corn cobs and jacket pota-
es to go with your grilled meats. Other-
se, wrap vegetables such as these in well-
uttered foil and place them directly among
e coals until they are done.

Vegetables, and cut-up fruit such as
heapple, can also be skewered on kebab
cks and grilled. A mixed vegetable kebab
ght include peppers, mushrooms, onion
d tomatoes. Certain breads, like pitta and
dian nan, taste delicious when heated for
couple of minutes on the grill and make
e perfect accompaniment.

ols of the Trade

e right utensils can be as essential to
rbecuing success as knowing how to light
e fire. Arm yourself with a good pair of
ngs, some skewers, protective oven-
oves and an apron. Spatulas, slices and
ngs are often sold as a set. Other acces-
ies you might like to consider if you are
nking of barbecuing regularly are some
m of shelter over the barbecue area so
t you can continue cooking in the event
a sudden shower; special spit and roaster
achments; a selection of different herbs
d spices to sprinkle on the coals; and a
w types of mustard and a couple of barbe-
e recipe books to expand your repertoire
yond sausages and burgers.

e End of the Day

important to close down the barbecue
perly when you have finished with it.

Lavender (*Lavandula*)   This popular herb is
as decorative as it is useful. This small
aromatic evergreen shrub grows to around
18–40in (45–100cm) and has spiky grey-
green foliage, a bushy habit and tiny but
attractive flowers. Some varieties such as
L. angustifolia 'Rosea' and *L. a.* 'Munstead'
have a particularly compact habit, which
makes them especially suited to growing in
containers – herbs such as this always look
good against terracotta. Lavender makes a
fine specimen plant but looks equally good in
an arrangement with other herbs, or when
clipped into a low hedge or topiary shape.

The more sophisticated machines simply
need to be switched off and wiped down,
but charcoal barbecues must be properly
extinguished. Air-vented models will go out
automatically once you close the vents and
put the cover on. Coals can be extinguished
using earth or sand – never use water – and
when they are completely cold, you can
empty them and clean the bowl and grid
ready for the next time.

Spring

● Sow your half-hardy annuals in a greenhouse or cold frame; when the ground is warm enough, sow hardy annuals outside. Later, tender annuals can be sown. Sow under glass any patio vegetables you have chosen to grow, such as cucumbers, lettuces, aubergines, sweet peppers and tomatoes. Keep the seedlings free from weeds and thin when they get too thick. Plant out in to patio growbags when the weather is warm enough.

Plastic growbags enable a wide range of tender vegetables to be grown on a sheltered patio.

● Alpines can be planted in your sink garden. Give it a check over, looking for pest infestation and firming in any plants that have been loosened by frost. Start watering regularly if the soil is dry. Trim plants such as aubretia and alyssum after flowering.
● New roses should be planted at the beginning of spring to give them a chance to become established. Prune any established roses and spray them before the pests get a hold. Plant under pot-grown standards with attractive carpeting plants to keep weeds down.
● Plant strawberries in strawberry barrels, growbags and tubs.

Put strawberry planters to use in spring by planting them with small flowering bulbs such as crocuses or scillas.

● Remove spring-flowering bulbs fr containers as they start to fade and rep them in the garden. Plant summ flowering bulbs in spare pots if there is room in your patio containers.
● Plant new evergreens. Prune shr where necessary.
● Trim wall-grown ivies.
● Remove patio furniture from store check its condition. Service any outdc lighting system and replace any fitme where necessary. Erect overhead scree etc, that have been stored away for winte

Summer

● Thin flower seedlings and plant ou required. Keep a bed of spares in the gar

A collection of slow-growing evergreens in attractive containers will maintain something of interest right through the year.

ll gaps in containers as required through season. Deadhead flowers regularly to plants blooming, but when finished, ove and replace immediately. Early atoes will need staking. Remove extra ots from the top and sides, as they ear, and keep plants well watered and As they fruit, crop while they are still ng and small.

Continue to trim and deadhead alpines equired, and water sink gardens care-. Keep them free from weeds and look or slugs. You can propagate from cut-if you need new plants.

Keep an eye open for any signs of se on roses and treat immediately. dhead daily and remove suckers. Tie up

Slugs and snails can totally destroy foliage plants, especially those that like damp conditions like hostas and ferns, so keep the patio area free from any decaying plant material and keep an eye open for slug or snail damage on plants.

Geraniums Free flowering, colourful and easy to care for, and with interesting foliage too – it is not surprising that geraniums are included in virtually every patio scheme. The hot reds and oranges are perfect for a sultry Mediterranean-style scheme, while the new pastel shades suit the subtlest modern planting plans. New hybrids bloom earlier yet will keep flowering until the first frosts. There are even varieties specially bred for use in hanging baskets, patio tubs and window-boxes, with strong basal branching, a free-flowering habit and well-marked foliage. The ivy-leaved varieties are particularly pretty.

● Treat any diseases or pest infestati immediately they are spotted. Use the m est remedy to begin with; try someth stronger only if the situation gets out hand.

● Remove unwanted strawberry runn and use them to propagate new plants if require more. When the crop is over, c away immediately.

● Lift tulips as soon as they have finis flowering and heel them into the gard Plant autumn-flowering bulbs in spare c tainers to provide something of interest r season.

● Deadhead azaleas and rhododendr and trim winter-flowering heathers. Pr shrubs as required and clip hedges. Pr wisteria. Water container-planted shr and trees diligently, and mulch the top the containers with pebbles, bark or pe reduce water evaporation on warm days

Autumn

● Clear away annual plants as they fi flowering. Continue to sow lettuce radish in the patio vegetable corner, ha cleared away tomatoes, peppers and s as they finish. Lift and pot a selectio herbs for overwintering indoors. Fill gaps in containers with ivies, winter pan and other suitable plants for providing interest through the winter.

● Plant any small bulbs in the al garden. Renew chippings and continu watch out for slug and snail damage. C erally tidy up. Plants susceptible to d may need covering with glass or plastic.

● Cut back unwanted new growth shrub roses. Finish pruning climbers ramblers.

● Keep the patio and pots clear of leaves.

● Order and plant bulbs for spring. early bulbs in special pots and conta for forcing for Christmas.

climbers and ramblers as they make new growth. If you are planning a new sink or rock garden, now would be a good time to make it.

● Many houseplants enjoy a little fresh air and sunshine if the weather is warm enough, and they can make an attractive extra feature when grouped together on a patio shelf or table. Take care that they do not get scorched and that they remain well fed and watered.

● Do not let any container-grown plants dry out during the hot weather. Mulch the top of the soil to prevent moisture loss, and install a simple automatic watering system if you do not have the time to water them yourself.

● When the nights start to shorten, clean up any barbecue equipment in preparation for the next year. There is nothing worse than finding it in a mess when you retrieve it from storage. Unless it is a permanent feature, pack it away in a cool, dry place.

Winter

● Dispose of any growbags and generally tidy up the patio area.
● Make necessary repairs to patio structures and restain or varnish timbers where required. Clean paving and disinfect, scrub timber decking free from moss with a stiff wire brush and apply a new coat of preservative if softwoods have been used.
● Make necessary repairs to patio furniture and put into store. Furniture that will stay out all winter may require a new coat of paint or preservative before the weather deteriorates.
● Mulching the top of shrub and tree containers will keep them free from weeds and conserve soil warmth.
● Cut back clematis and prune other shrubs which carry their flowers on the young wood. When the blooms of winter-flowering jasmine have finished, the flowering stems should be cut back almost to the old wood. Remove a few of the older stems at the base.
● Install a small heater for any fish that might be overwintering in the pool.
● If you have a moving-water feature, keep the pump running in winter to prevent the water's freezing. Otherwise, shut it down and get it serviced. This is particularly important for above-ground pumps.
● Remove less frost-resistant patio containers to a more sheltered spot and wrap in hessian or newspaper to prevent cracking or shattering when temperatures drop.
● Browse through the seed catalogues and pick out your colour schemes for next year's stunning patio display!

onifers Dwarf and slow-growing conifers
ake excellent additions to patio pots and
anting beds. They require very little
aintenance yet look good all year round,
aking a fine permanent background to
easonal plantings. They come in an amazing
nge of shapes and colours from blue, green
d gold to silver, and from domes, spires
d balls to pyramids. *Chamaecyparis*
wsoniana alone can offer a choice of golden
omes, green columns, or grey, purple and
en white foliage. There are also compact
nus varieties in shades of grey and blue, and
een or bright yellow varieties of *Thuja* with
ovely bronze colour in the winter.

Tie up any new growth on climbing
nts. You can also plant new trees and
ubs, providing the soil is not frozen.
Clean up pots and remove any dead
terial from the patio area.
Keep patio ponds free from leaves and
er plant debris to avoid fouling the
er. Cover with net if necessary.
Rampant aquatic plants should be thin-
 to more manageable proportions.
en required, drain out and clean the
ole pool, taking care not to damage the
r. Plants and fish can convalesce in a
 or in another pool in the garden,
viding the water is not chlorinated. Do
reintroduce them into the main pool
 the water here has neutralized too.

GLOSSARY

Acid   Having a pH below 7.
Aggregate   Stony particles mixed with cement, sand and water to make concrete.
Alfresco   Outdoors.
Alkaline   Having a pH above 7.
Alpine   Plants that are adapted to the extreme temperatures and thin, stony soil of high altitudes.
Angle grinder   A machine capable of cutting stone sets and slabs.
Awning   Stretched sheet of fabric or canvas affording shade or shelter.

Basket weave   An arrangement of bricks, timber, threads and so on to resemble the woven pattern of a basket.
Bond   The arrangement of bricks.
Butyl   A type of rubber often used as a pool-lining material.

Coach bolts   Heavy-duty bolts used for timber.
Cobbles   Rounded stones or pebbles set in concrete to make a paved surface.
Compost   Potting mixture made either from peat or coconut fibre (known as soil-less compost); or from sterilized soil (known as loam compost).
Container plant   A plant which has been grown and sold in a pot or other container. It can be planted at almost any time of the year because root disturbance is minimal.
Countersinking   Sinking the head of a bolt or screw below the timber's surface.
Course   A continuous, usually horizontal layer of building material such as bricks.
Crazy paving   Random arrangement of broken paving materials.
Cultivar   A variety of a natural plant species that is maintained through cultivation.

Datum peg   Measuring peg to which all other pegs refer.
Deadheading   Removing dead or dying blooms.
Deciduous   Plants that lose their foliage annually.

Decking   A continuous timbered surfa which is raised off the ground.
Dormant   When a plant temporarily sto growing, usually in winter.
Dowel   A plug or peg used to join t pieces of timber.
Drystone wall   A wall constructed fro stone without mortar.

Evergreen   Plants which retain th foliage throughout the year.

Fertilizer   A chemical (organic or in ganic) that provide a plant with food.
Focal point   The centre of attention feature which commands most attention.
Fungicide   A chemical (organic or in ganic) used to control fungal diseases.

Gazebo   A type of open summer-house pavilion.
Genus   A botanic category denotin family of related plant species.
Geometric   Composed of simple, reg forms such as circles, rectangles, trian and so on.

Half-hardy   A plant that is usually kille frost.
Hardcore   Broken brick, stones and o rubble used as a foundation for concrete
Hardy   A plant which is tolerant of temperatures.
Herbaceous plants   Non-woody or stemmed plants, usually border perenni
Herring-bone   A pattern used in b work and textiles, where two or more r of short parallel strokes slant in alter directions to create a series of par zigzags.
Hibachi   A type of portable barbecue.
Humidity   The amount of moisture tained in the air.
Hybrid   A plant resulting from a c between two genetically dissimilar viduals.
Hypertufa   Mixture of sphagnum m

d and cement, which is used to cover
disguise glazed sinks used as con-
ers.

cticide A chemical (organic or inorga-
which kills insects.

dscaping Laying out a garden, usually
nitation of natural features.
n A good, fertile soil.

roclimate The atmospheric conditions
ing to a small group.
tar A mixture of cement or lime (or
) with sand to create a bond between
ks or stones.
ch Material spread on the surface of
oil around a plant to conserve moisture
to suppress weeds.

ntation Position in relation to the
ts of a compass – in other words, north,
n, east and west.

cle A flower spike.
The partially decomposed plant
rial traditionally used to improve soil,
vhich has recently been replaced by
materials such as coconut fibre due to
ecline of boglands.
nnials Long-lived plants which
ar each year.
ola A horizontal trellis or framework,
etimes creating a walkway and
ned as a support for climbing plants.
ing The cement between bricks or
s.
us Having the ability to absorb water.
ound The stage when a plant's roots
ramped in its container.
ng on Placing a plant in a new, larger
hen it outgrows its old one.

Propagate To reproduce plants by seeds,
cuttings and so on.

Screed board A tool used for levelling
mortar.
Shuttering Temporary arrangement of
planks used to contain concrete whilst wet.
Species The subdivisions of a genus.
Spirit level A tool with a tube containing
liquid, which indicates whether a vertical
or horizontal surface is level.
Straightedge A tool used to obtain a perfect right angle.
Subsoil The layer of soil beneath the surface soil and above the bed rock.
Symmetrical Having two sides which are
perfectly balanced.
Systemic A pesticide or fungicide which
spreads through all parts of the plant without damaging it.

Tender A plant which requires protection
from low temperatures.
Terracotta Hard, unglazed, russet-red
earthenware.
Topiary Trimming or training trees and
shrubs into ornamental shapes.
Topsoil The fertile soil on top of the
ground.
Transpire To lose water.
Trellis A structure of latticework which is
useful when growing climbing plants.

Variegated Having leaves which are
marked in a secondary colour.
Versailles planter A style of plant container featuring wood or fibreglass panels
raised on four feet and sometimes with
finial decorations.

Width gauge Piece of timber used to
space slabs or bricks evenly.

INDEX